ROBERT ZALLER
ISLANDS

ISLANDS

Robert Zaller

SOMERSET HALL PRESS
Boston, Massachusetts

© Copyright 2006 Robert Zaller
Published by Somerset Hall Press
416 Commonwealth Avenue, Suite 612
Boston, Massachusetts 02215
www.somersethallpress.com

Cover design: Kimon Rethis

Acknowledgments:

"Aphrodite of Kythera": *Lives of the Poet* (New York: Barlenmir House, 1974).
"The Islands Appear": *For Empedocles* (Athens: European Arts Center, 1996).
"Rock Island." "Exile Island." "Among the Others." "Again the Sea." "Keros." *Philadelphia Poets*, 11, 2 (2005).

Library of Congress Cataloging-in-Publication Data

Zaller, Robert.
 Islands : poems / by Robert Zaller.
    p. cm.
 ISBN 0-9774610-2-5 (alk. paper)
 I. Title.
PS3576.A37I85 2006
811'.5'4--dc22

                              2006017305

CONTENTS

For Lili, forever

ISLANDS

Blaze here comes to a white wing, everywhere that air
blows. Through this gap pierced, skylight.

- André du Bouchet

APHRODITE OF KYTHERA

Here a god fell out of the sky
  and where his living groin struck water
a goddess calved from the waves:
  such is the wise economy of myth.
A whirlpool of light marks the spot
  fixed on mariners' maps with a golden Ω
as if here at last the proud and militant sea
  consented to bear a name.

Today on this outcast rock
  above the pale-haired fields
neither worshipped nor profaned for centuries
  I seek the wild goddess with disordered hair
tempest-witch of Time and Water
  the living statue beneath the sea.
Home, I rest. My love has left
  a plate of olives. I turn the door

and see her, hair spread wildly, blackly back
  against the pillow, her face
a great staring plaque, unfocused and all-seeing,
  expressionless in its intensity.
I smile in fear. My love smiles back,
  human, lovely, returned to herself.
But I am trembling. For I have seen
  the living mask beneath the green-eyed sea.

THE ISLANDS APPEAR

In the evening the islands appear
faint blue incisions on the parchment of night
coming each day to live their hour
between the red sun's fall and the evening star.
Sea and sky are perfect,
the dying sun marries them.
Pure volume, lucid height.
Yet without islands there is no solace.
Born under the plunge of the sun, their frailty,
like ours, dies with the light.
Their single flaw makes distance real.
They are the riddle that solves the night.

BEFORE ISLANDS

The fret of motion
stirs the world
to being.
The gull's eye,
that never sleeps,
is its centerless center.
It sees hunger,
feigns a mouth.
Hunger is aloft,
an eye, a beak,
raging at the sea.

All this was before islands,
before the first cliff
that shouldered up
and snagged the sky.

WAVE AND GULL

The wind blows from the west,
the wavecrests surge, dip, fail.
The gulls ride them like anxious herdsmen,
coasting the difficult air.
The waves are in their beaks,
the whiteness, the terrible whiteness.

THE FIRST TEAR

A flat sea, one undulant blue
as if to illustrate
the principle of motion
a sky with nothing to do
but host the sun
a horizon ruled
between two plenitudes:
this was the world's first day
the wet and the dry
two shades of the same color.
Creation wanted nothing
but its flaw, the mote
in the eye of All. How then
to secrete its own imperfection
how divide Lesser to lesser
what crack in the sky
what faltering thought
again and again
but never the same twice?
Rock meant bird, bird meant sail,
the shuffle of dust.
God saw, and he wept.
The first tear foretold the rest.

ELEMENTS

Rock, thistle, lichen, isle—
the fingering wave, the dart
of the lizard, the lingering
spiral of the gull that plucks
the breast of the sea—
these are the elements on which
the wind takes its pleasure,
first of all raptors,
God's word unbroken, a roar
and a stillness, commandment
and silence, winding itself
about the bull's ear like
a wreath of flies, sweeping
the unclean altar, scattering
the ash of sacrifice:

the elements alone remain.
They have outlived their creator,
whose cry echoes in the landscape,
locked in stone.

AMONG THE OTHERS

The island rises from the sea
like a fresh-baked loaf of bread
and takes its place among the others.
So morning comes. Nothing disturbs
the blue dimension but those tiny
white brows that seem raised in surprise
over the vast unopened eye of being.

STILL HOT FROM CREATION

The waves are busy here,
nothing else. Gray rock,
low shrub, roots
that thirst. The sun
comes over the crown
of the hill,
searches, and goes down.
What is night here?
Yet nothing lacks.
Men made idols once,
and left. Thistle grows,
and the uncarved rock,
still hot from creation
though cold to the touch
holds its station.

The gulls dive
parting the day
again and again.

PASSING ISLANDS

They lie like shields
stacked to the horizon.
Sail to one. See if it is possible.
The rock at waterline is gray,
giving way to the sea's
insistent surprise. We cannot stay,
though it seems made
for our step.

The islands rise,
a halt in being,
a question posed
between the sentence of the sea
and the pardon of the sky.

AFTERNOON OF THE ISLANDS

It's the hour of erasure
when blue flows into blue
the sun strikes us dumb
the horizon wavers
the birds disappear.
Nothing survives
the crush of being
but there an island rises
gray cape on a matador's point
another and another
like constellations coming out at night.
The light won't win today
nor the dark
as long as the islands
cast javelins at the sky.

THE ELEMENTS THEMSELVES

Beyond the blue sea
the scrim of mountains
stage and curtain in one
the waves chatter
the sail tacks
for the shore.
The busy gulls
decipher the scroll
of this day
the cypresses walk
like Druids threatening the sea,
or chanting, wave by wave,
its holy name.
No human actor:
only the elements themselves,
wide in their speech
grave in their song
filled with their poem.

What are the islands to me,
what is Greece?

- H. D.

ROCK ISLAND

Donoussa

Rock island
your scaly plates
loose underfoot
the wind lowing
in your sullen harbor.
Your peasants plant stones
and reap headlands.
Tumuli sprout
on your low foreshores.
Dry roots snare the ground.
The sea cuts teeth in you,
you marry its spittle.
The dreams of marble are elsewhere,
the athletes in the gold of their sweat
the thoughtful sculptors, the sheaves of wheat.
Elsewhere the academies,
the earnest fortresses of reason.
You are too severe for reason.
You offer no prophecy,
only a bitter spring bubbles once a year,
the fault in your issue.
The axe finds nothing to cut.
It saws at the wind.
The gulls cast their empty eyes
at the sea.
You are nothing but strict refusal,
whittled horizon.
Black stone, gray stone.
Rock island.

EXILE ISLAND

The powder sky seems to sift the dust,
there is none. Only rock and storm,
storm and distance, winter's pasture
on a foreland where nothing lives
but lava beneath stone,
nothing waits but endurance itself
and the bird of time passes, repasses,
weaving a perpetual sky.

      You have the arrow
and it festers in your flesh
you are a stench for miles around,
incurable. You are the destined hero
and the archers will fetch you,
glory lies before you on a spread plain.
This the god in the serpent and the scorpion
tells you, this the thistle whispers
as it snags your unbound wound.
But you have won patience,
silence, and the pity of nothing.
You need nothing more. The wound
becomes a weather, your lameness
a bird's flight, your agony
the rock's temper in the storm,
you are the cautery and cure, the standing cliff
beyond hope. The arrow is released.
The archers when they come
find no trace that any man has been here.

KEROS

Gulls describe a cliff
weaving it back and forth
with the strong thread
of a sail

A surf of hills
makes its lunge
against a wilder blue

They say a goatherd
lives on Keros, or a monk.
I like to think
he is the harpist who plays
the mad music of the wind.

THE REHEARSAL

Dawn. The first cast of silver
on the bare blue shield
the islands rough-shouldering
themselves into the sky
the first gull hunting the wave
the sun's angry eye
setting watchfires on the sea.
Gold hastens to the rock.
It is all one chord of light
struck from the silent gong,
rehearsing another day.

THE VOICE OF THE SEA

The voice of the sea is great
at night. It hurdles the dark
like a flood in the valley
and only the island's bulk,
thin as the walls of a dream,
holds it back. Day restores
the bounded world, limned by light,
patrolled by wind. Night belongs
to the chaos of Old Ocean,
that surges through the salt veins
that branch from silence to silence,
star to star. That drowns the heavens
and spares only the rock
straining to rise, unshaken by night,
unmastered by dawn.

THE LAMPS HOLD THE STARS IN THEIR HANDS

Heaven lets down its wings.
Look carefully, see the threads.
The wing seeks the eye of the wave
with a needle of fire.
Look carefully, see the rain of light
that falls and rises, falls and rises,
instant in the cloudless sky.
Thus weaves the world, filament to filament,
like ropes let down, stiff with salt,
like nets that float, blooming,
in search of the sea.
The islands sway like the crowns of tottering empires.
The ladders of heaven drop to us
rung by rung, salvation on each.

At night,
the lamps hold the stars in their hands.

THE WAY

The way rock folds upon rock
valley upon valley
the way shadow falls
a blade between them
the way the hills keep their silence
no matter how the wind urges speech
the way the unrung bell resounds

the way the island thinks its solitude
through a dream of morning
the way the sea thirsts for rock
the way a cliff anchors the sky
the way blue answers blue
the way the grasses flee without stirring
the way the bird shakes the tamarisk tree

until it bursts into song
and a lone gull, blinking back
the air, leads the penitent islands
one by one to the horizon.

DAYS OF 2003

Up the marbled track
from the busy street
silence falls like a blow.
The sea tirelessly cancels
the rock, and beyond
the jutting cape
a white sail stiffens,
far off, far nearer
to that island than this one
but still, perceptibly closer.
The strong wind
pulls at the rock life,
the green-gold gorse,
the stalks that crack in the sun,
the lizard taking up his stations
one by one. The ants file
around the stone that sits
like a Mycenaean burial chamber
in their path.
They carry gold tassels.
How they toil.
The wave drives up
into the suck of the cave.
I write this poem on the rock.
The wind tears it away.

THE STONES

The stones bear the day's weight
patiently. The rough grasses
feed on light, the bush and bramble,
beetle and lizard, all the island
affords of native life. These things
are greedy for day, grateful for night.
The stones wear the heat and the cold
as a garment turned either way.
The rain does not cool them,
the sun's chisel has no tooth.
Men split them into axes,
heap them for fences, raise them
for temples, lay sacrifices
beneath them. They do not resist
and do not care. They have suffered
their journey already, and rest accomplished.
Their fate is to exist and their work is to decay
into grains a god's sandal prints,
to be borne on the wind and dropped in the sea
and never cease from kind.
The lichen try them, and fall off.
They fill my cup of silence
to the brim, their long watch
sees me home.

LEAVE ONLY HEAVEN

The hills unbend to the sea.
North, the great island
gives its flanks to the sun
the blue shadows retreating,
the dawn mist rising.
A rough wind tugs
the forelock of the island,
shaking the pale grass
and the stunted trees.
Nothing grows well
but the stones,
the stiff wealth of the island.
They are the only thing plentiful.
The sun quarries them anew.

Oh, there are humans, too,
few, but more than needed.
They heap the stones up
to make a thing called property.
The island rests easily enough
with that. The islands all gather
on the forenoon, like boats
resting their oars
on the enkindled sea.
The horizon is a far guess from here
where blue form rests
on a silver salver

and the plenitude of being
is so full
that a drop more of water
a grain more of sand
would make it all vanish
and leave only heaven.

PROPHETS GO MAD

The sea wears these islands
like a bone bracelet
on the milk-white morning
and nothing moves.
The crickets put up
and take down
their walls of sound.
Bells stream through the valley.
Somewhere a motor thrums,
whether on water or land
I cannot tell. This rock
faces me like a skull,
the sunken eyepit and tusked nostrils
of some ancient mastodon.
Nothing has greatly changed;
a few revolutions of life.
I climb with the sun,
parting the domes of the hills.
Prophets, I know, go mad
in the hills. But if I could dwell
one day above the human
not to smell history or taste it
how gladly I would come home to you
with wild figs for the hearth
and a stone in my pocket for luck.

ROCK SKEINS

The rock skeins lie offshore
bone-white, gray, and black,
resisting all color
but not the wave's green surge.
Deep-caverned bays it carves,
spurs and hillocks,
caves and arches.
Bone oracles, the future
writes on them, and the sand shore
fulfills the prophecy.
Here and there ice plants
poke through like desert oases.
Here a dolphin sports, a lion rests,
a centaur dreams.
Noon raises both arms.
The future arrives.

THE GIVEN

The given: stone. And sea, soil, stars.
And that vault of heaven (shall we say)
that holds day and night
in a tide that breaks on no shore
but the sea. We cannot conjure
depth from light, and so the Philosopher
says all space is illusion. Nothing arrives
at its destined end. How does the light
flood us, we who do not drown, how
does it strike us, we who do not fall?
We, too, are the manifold, and our illusion
is that we stand. Grit grinds our feet,
the beginning and the end of stone,
the prick of being. We are that stone.
Flux fills and empties us,
the gated sea keeps its secrets,
swinging on the blue hinge.
What is given: appearance and void,
the island's eruption, the clamor
of wings that tears the cloth
and bears its prey to rapture . . .

And if an island moves is it the same
island but in a new place?

- William Stafford

THE STORY OF ISLANDS

One day an island crawled up from the sea
sucked and folded on itself
licked itself clean
crouched on the horizon
tawny as Rousseau's desert lion.
The sea is not a desert
though it is great and empty
the island is not a lion
though its flanks are supple
and its jaws are powerful.
The sky has the last word.
It does not like metaphors
and it erases
all the sea has made.
This is the story of islands.
They mutter darkly at night
and leap joyfully as dolphins
at daybreak.
The sky docs not like that metaphor either
but the sea is full of them
and so there are islands.

THE ISLAND WITHOUT A NAME

The islands hereabout
have many names
the dower of many conquests,
many tongues, many gods.
This one has none.
It lies across the bay—
you can hardly miss it—
long and dragon-tailed,
with a scatter of ruins
and the scar of some roads
invisible in the glare of noon.
From this island, too,
it fills the horizon
you can't escape it
try as you will
from this cliff or that.
It hasn't less beauty
than any other island.
The waves approach it
no less eagerly,
the gulls take it by storm.
No one ever mentions it;
it has no name.
The fishermen creep quietly
toward it and take their catch;
you can see their lamps
and the tips of their cigarettes.
No one makes landfall,

nor does anyone speak;
they work the nets.

The ruins are recent.
You'll still see bedding,
a stool, a ledger,
a stone on which
someone scratched a human face,
not too long ago.
But no one goes there now.
The island has a name, they say,
but no one remembers it.
All islands have names,
many names; it is their nature.
They came up from the sea
and the race of man greeted them.
Old bedding, a stool,
a silent knife.
This island was interrupted.
It has a name, but in a file.
No boat stops here,
no one keeps the roads up,
nothing grows in the fields.
Someone knows the name
of this island,
but no one hereabouts.
Some god lived here,
all islands have gods.
Perhaps his footprint
is still alive on it,
somewhere in the hills.

Perhaps he'll come down
and reclaim it,
open the sanctuaries,
waken the oracles.
But no man will go there.
It's too far, they say, too near.
The currents are treacherous,
the omens are bad.
Besides, this island has no name.
No one goes
to an island without a name.

THE ISLAND OF THE BLIND

On the island of the blind
one feels for the light.
It's like the last impulse
before creation, the imminent
surge of glory.
The islanders are sure-footed
as goats, hopping from rock
to rock, ledge to ledge.
They know every step
of their dark shore
with an animal's instinct,
an owner's love.
Beauty gives them no pause,
shadow no hesitation.
They know that night
is when the fish come out,
and set their nets.
Their harvest is very full.
They have lived here long,
and kill all intruders.
Do not think
they fail to sense you.
Otherwise, they are perfectly
at peace. They have no quarrel,
and their eyes are bright.
Sight is the only misfortune
they can think of.
Once a god cursed them

with it. The sea's expanse
appalled them. They put out
each other's eyes, and buried
the flints. They lit a fire
it cheered them not to see.

On the island of the blind
birds fly freely, and the wave
smacks the cape. Day and night
make a single monotony.
The horizon has long since crumbled.
The stars raise their torches
in vain. The blind
lack for nothing, and nothing
is given them.

The god thinks:
I will find another island.

THE ISLAND WITH A CLOUD

One day a cloud appeared
among the islands. It chose one,
and stayed. The island
was neither pretty nor large
(well, I mean exceptional,
for all these islands
are beautiful, their shapes
are comely). It had neither
philosopher nor strong man,
and its women were beautiful
only as all women are. Its goats
gave no more milk, nor ran
more freely, and the stars
above it were exactly the same
as elsewhere. Yet the cloud
chose it and no other.
You must know our islands,
in these latitudes blue
is the only color except
for what the sun grants us
on its way to the underworld,
the gold cliffs and the hollows
where night gathers its purple folds.
Only the wavecrests are white,
and the first, forbidden light
of dawn. Our seers debated earnestly.
Some felt the cloud a sign
of blessing, some a curse. Others

believed the cloud had made
no choice at all, but merely hung
in the absence of wind. The winds
came, but did not dislodge it.
Some gathered in its shadow
to pray, others shunned it
as a place of evil. When a she-goat
bore a deformed human creature
with two horns, the archipelago
voted to move on. The island
was left alone with its cloud.
Years later, a shipwrecked sailor
sought refuge on it. But there
was neither cloud nor island
to be seen, only the expanse
of the everlasting sea.

THE LOST ISLAND

The island stretched its pale finger
toward the dying sun
but could not save it.
A trick of perspective
perched its last gleam
atop it like a bloodless ruby.
Thus the island died too
in a slow summation of blue.
All night it sailed, a ghost freighter.
One by one, the others joined it.
Our vessels, becalmed, took their places.
At dawn they returned,
and our engines kicked.
Only now and then
an island is lost
and nothing will call it back.
It keeps sailing, perhaps,
a sliver of blue finitude
that belongs to neither sea nor sky.
The day moon hunts it
to no avail. Yet men will swear
they've seen it in a dolphin's wake,
or a wave whose tongue searches
its unattainable crests. It's only
a lost island, it will turn up
any day now, here or there.

THE ISLAND THAT FELL FROM THE SKY

All islands, of course,
are waveborn,
but this one fell
from the sky
and failed to burn
in the upper heavens
like a rare meteor
transfixing itself
or a bone flung
into the famished sea.

THE ISLAND OF THE DAMNED

More and more arrive
each day. Yet the island
is never crowded, for no man
greets another. Sweet
is the solitude of the damned.
They cross and recross
the little square with the plane tree.
No one sees another in his path.
They sit in the café,
shoulder to shoulder,
and study the coffee grounds
to read the future.
There is none.
The next boat arrives.
It is not a bad life,
here at the meridian.
The sun rises and sets
at the same hour,
the same fish reappears
on the plate.
The eyes of the damned
are glazed with contentment.
They neither blink nor close.
Once in a great while
a shrill murmur rises
from them in place of speech.
It is a reflex,
the island doctor says.

He sees no patients.
Lizards dart among the damned,
snakes come out at night.
Harmless, they need no other
guardian, no boundary
but the wind's echo, the sky's void,
the stride of the gull-swift wave.

THE ISLAND OF SEVEN WINDS

This island is crossed by seven winds.
Each has its own cry.
The high and piercing ones
sing through a bird's beak,
the low ones sweep the ground
tugging the brush to life.
Nothing feeds here
except the birds
and they are all tongues of wind.
The rest is stone,
which is without appetite
and unmoved by wind.
This is what the wind wants
when it wants islands—
to hear all its orchestras
sound above silence
far from the chatter
and frivolity of the sea.

.   .. nor can Being exceed
or fall short of itself,
          an inviolate whole
equal to itself in every direction,
uniformly present within its bounds.

                    - Parmenides

THE SILENCE OF THE ISLAND

I walk
the silence
of the island.
The west
fills with light.
Each stone
takes its benediction.
A tethered goat
bleats on the hill.
A bird
startles a tree
with three fierce notes.
The wind drones,
and the sea,
working its passage,
rests an oar
on the rush of time.
All this
is the silence
of the island,
the core
of its dreaming,
the secret stillness.
Here speech
sinks into itself,
the finally unsaid.

THE RANSOM OF HEAVEN

A noon haze
becalms the island.
The sun drives
its stakes into the ground,
raising the tent
of the sky.
The wind has dropped.
The sea lies prone.
The lizard seeks his rock,
the tourist his café.
A white sail flies up,
all form rests in fire
and none dares gaze
at the ransom of heaven.

THE GULL'S SHADOW

I saw the gull's shadow
race along the sands
and looked up
to see the gull.
There was nothing
there. He had disappeared
into flight.

THE GULLS, THEIR CRY

The gulls are mostly
silent, but they have
their angry cry,
letting out its own syllable,
riding it hard to the end.
One circles me,
crying, as if trying
to settle the world,
or solve it.
The earthbound
have no such language
their voices do not carry
far.

  The gull
circles again,
repeating its note.
It settles on a tower,
profiling the sky.
A second settles
beside it, not inches apart.
Both stay awhile,
perfectly still.

The world holds its breath.

One flies away.

HUNGER

The birds watch the earth
with a hungry eye,
likewise the sea.
God does not judge
more sternly.
They plummet on salvation
seizing the world
into midair
to remake it
as a beak, a wing, an eye,
the fixed and final form
of our perfection.

FOUR ELEMENTS

Up the road to the Hopperesque
gas pump, right in the middle
of nowhere. I look at
the long fall to the sea
dirt tracks ebbing out,
broken walls, the ruin
of a house. Down where
the hills twist to an end
the waves come flying ashore,
marshaled by the horizon
herded by the wind.
You can hear nothing
but its roar, a thousand whips
cracked at once.
It fills the immensity of air
that has nothing to do
but contain it. Stone has
nothing to say, the wind
says nothing but itself.
No smoking, the gas pump says,
sensibly. What would we do
here with fire?

THE BIRDS

The birds live
in every element,
air, water, earth.
The phoenix lives in fire.
Think of that.
Even the gods
have no such dominion.

THE CATCH

The boat heads toward shore.
The gull follows it.
There's a catch,
but the man won't share it.
The gull feeds in the wake
and veers off
to the open sea.

THE WAVES KNOW BETTER

The wind saws the island
in half. It whines in fury.
The island shrugs.
It shakes out its trees
like holiday flags.
Make sport of the waves,
it says. *You can do nothing here.*
But the waves know better,
showing their whitecaps.
Give us time, they say. *Give us time.*

WIND AND STARS

The stars are fire, we know,
but have cold wisdom too.
The ancients thought them fixed,
we as flung,
like pebbles against a roof.
Let them wander if they will.
Here the wind thinks
its one thought,
the bright torches
branch with night.
A creature finds its burrow
under a rustling tree.
By this measure
we guess at distance
and draw breath
to climb the eventual sky.

NIGHT

The sun sets.
The wind hurries gold
through the long grasses.
The sea rests anchor
under the rock.
The great birds rise,
whetting their beaks.
One sail passes the harbor.
The stars shake their plumage,
like dancers awaiting their cue.
Night
veers from a wing.

AGAIN THE SEA

Thasos

Again the sea
the black ash of Gomorrah
settling on it
the blackened cone
floating to mate
with the leaf
and go with the tide

Now the black apples
that hang from our boughs
wither to the pips
when we pluck them
long after
they will explode in the earth
the ash will come down
again the sea

A wave goes over the earth
without breaking
and returns to itself
an oath scratches itself on glass
and the stumps of the hills
turn, on black crutches,
to march all the way
to the wind.

THE ARCHIPELAGO

From here
one can see
all the islands—
well, almost all—
sitting like plums
on the silvered sea.
That one, there,
is the island of seven winds,
guarded by its invisible ramparts,
where neither man nor viper
has ever roamed.
Over there, on another,
is the watchtower
that relayed the fall of Troy—
but that was long ago,
and ancient wars
are a fable.
Each island has a story,
but what's important
is that they begin in fire
and end in stone.
That is: they begin
in the mind's eye
and end in dream.
The dream alone is real.

ULYSSES' RETURN

Ulysses sits on this step
like an old fisherman
broken by the sea.
He has loved all islands
but hates the one
that keeps him.
He scans the horizon
but on this dull sea
there is never a sail.
He should rest content
with his adventures
but he'd willingly
turn swine again
for one last island,
even the one that wants
no hero and knows no god.
Any sort of island will do—
friendless, uncompanioned—
as long as it craves the wind
and bears the sea.

THE ISLAND EATER

Nisophagos ise, says Minas,
spreading his big fishcatcher's
fingers and smiling
the slow smile of his sixty years.
You are an island eater. It's true.
I go from one to another,
always looking for the last,
the perfect island. They are all
perfect, but each in its own way.
So I go on to the next,
and the next. One day
I'll take the last trip
and see them all together
like fish on a string.
Until then, show them
to me one by one,
each by each.

THE LAST ISLAND

What, then, is truth?
The answer is not
in any word of man.
Believe no son of man
who tells you so,
nor any son of God.
Believe in no god either
except to hone terror
or sharpen ecstasy.
Men want to know
when they forget to live,
to possess what they fail
to enjoy. The still serpent,
alert to bask or strike,
knows both. He is
the emblem of your truth.

It is our last day here.
The city of lies
with its glorious temple
awaits us. Below,
the sea slurs its syllables,
the gull marks
the wave's white progress.
A lone tree nods
to the wind's flutes,
its reply inaudible
in the cicada's drone.

The nets of silence
draw in their catch.
The emperor sun ascends
his throne. The horizon
imagines itself between
one blue and another.
A third one rides it,
a stutter in the air,
a sketch flawed by doubt.
There is nothing further
to be seen. The last island
is the truth.

About the Author

Robert Zaller, poet, critic, and historian, is the author of four previous verse collections: *The Year One, Lives of the Poet, Invisible Music,* and *For Empedocles.* His other books include *The Cliffs of Solitude: A Reading of Robinson Jeffers,* and he is, with Lili Bita, the translator of *Thirty Years in the Rain: The Selected Poetry of Nikiforos Vrettakos* (Somerset Hall Press). Stanford University Press will publish his *The Discourse of Legitimacy in Early Modern England* in 2007. He is Professor of History at Drexel University.

446501

Made in the USA